CUP
CAKE
PARTY
BOOK

Published by
General Foods Corporation
White Plains, New York
Produced by
Special Marketing Division
Dell Publishing Company, Inc.

CONTENTS

PAGE

INTRODUCTION. 4
SOME BASIC CAKE TALK 6
PERFECT PARTY PLOT 10
CAKE, FROSTING RECIPES. 14

CUT-UP CAKES

AIRPLANE 24
ANGEL. 28
THE BEAUTIFUL BALLOON. 32
BUTTERFLY. 36
CABIN CRUISER 40
CANNONBALL EXPRESS 44
THE CHRISTMAS TREE. 48
THE CLOWN 52
CUDDLY BUNNY 56
DAISY. 60
EASY BUNNY. 64
THE FLOWER CART 68
THE HAPPY HOUSE. 72
A PAIR OF HEARTS 76
THE PERFECT DOLL 80
PERKY TURKEY. 84
THE RACER 88
SAILBOAT 92
SANTA CLAUS. 96
SPACE SHIP. 100
ALL STAR SPORTS PAGE 104
TEDDY BEAR. 108
THE TIGER. 112
UMBRELLA 116
THE WITCH 120
WOOFY DOG. 124

INTRODUCTION

Party Time is cake time. Not just any cake but a super special W O W of a cake — The Cut-Up Cake.

For a perfect party go the Cut-Up route. These whimsical wonderful cakes are not just for children — but for everyone.

The clue to the cake selection is in the occasion. There's a just-right Cut-Up Cake for all kinds of celebrations — birthdays, holidays, special days unlimited.

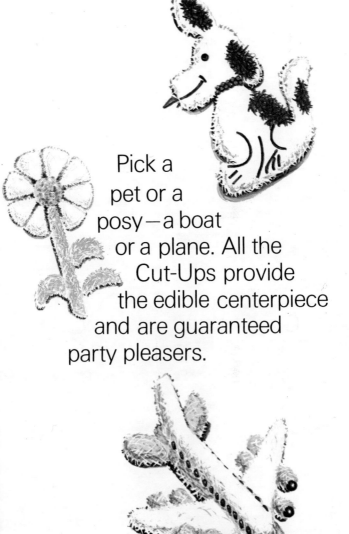

Pick a
pet or a
posy—a boat
or a plane. All the
Cut-Ups provide
the edible centerpiece
and are guaranteed
party pleasers.

and now SOME BASIC CAKE TALK

Cut-Ups are a breeze to make
—no special tools or molds are needed.

The cake you cut up can be made from your favorite recipe or from a 2-layer size cake mix. Most Cut-Ups begin with 8- or 9-inch layers, or a 13 x 9-inch cake. Select the cake flavor of your choice and check the baking directions, making sure that the cake can be baked in the specified size pan. (Baking instructions for special size pans are included with the recipes.)

Follow package or recipe directions carefully. Note the baking time and oven temperature given for the size cake you are preparing.

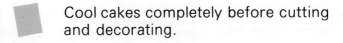
Cool cakes completely before cutting and decorating.

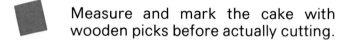

Measure and mark the cake with wooden picks before actually cutting.

Shaded portions of diagrams indicate pieces of cake not used in assembling Cut-Ups. (If there are children around, leftover pieces will disappear fast— otherwise use cake crumbs or cubes in combination with puddings or as topping on canned or frozen fruits.)

Assemble all cake pieces on a serving tray before frosting, unless instructions specify otherwise. If you don't have a tray large enough, cover heavy cardboard with foil.

To keep serving tray free of frosting and coconut, tuck strips of wax paper beneath assembled cake pieces before frosting. When you've finished, carefully slide these strips away, along with spilled frosting and coconut.

First frost pieces together to hold; then frost all cut edges, leaving tops and uncut edges for last. Patterns cut from wax paper, laid over frosting, will help keep coconut off those parts of the cake where it isn't wanted.

Going to travel with the cake? Then place it in a sturdy, shallow cardboard box not too much larger than the tray holding the Cut-Up. A few wooden picks inserted into the cake will keep plastic wrap or foil from smearing the frosting. And you'll find it easier to carry candies separately, and finish decorating the cake later.

THE PERFECT PARTY PLOT

How do you feel about parties? Exhausted and defeated at the very thought of entertaining—or ready and eager at the slightest excuse. There are, of course, times when the responsibilities of parenthood, friendship, community, and business life necessitate giving a party whether you want to or not!

But surely the best time to give a party is when you really want to entertain—when you look forward to enjoying yourself and bringing pleasure to your guests. The party sparked by personal enthusiasm is the one with a head start lead to success.

So—You Want To Give A Party—

celebrating an important family event, a birthday, an anniversary, graduation or special party for friends—START WITH A PLAN.

I. Write Things Down

What kind of a party will it be? When and where will it take place? Who will be invited?

The kind of party helps determine the time and date. It's a good idea to check with a few people to make sure that the date you have selected does not conflict with another already planned event.

Be realistic about space, budget, and your own way of life. If you live in a small house or apartment and are most at ease in a casual atmosphere, don't try to invite a crowd of 50 people for a formal dinner. Why try to do the impossible when with a little thought and imagination you can do your own special kind of party and do it well.

II. The Logic of Lists

Make a guest list. Invitations can be phoned or mailed, but keeping track of invited guests is essential. Allow plenty of time for guests to respond. Remembering at the last minute that you forgot to call someone back (busyline—no answer) can be embarrassing for you and disappointing to the left-out person.

For children's parties, let them help you with the guest list and invitations. This will help to make it their party—not yours.

Make a shopping list. Write a complete menu plan including all the items you plan to serve. Review recipes checking carefully to see if you have all ingredients. Last minute races to the store for a forgotten item are time consuming and wearying. Include on your shopping lists special party equipment such as napkins, favors, and decorations. You may now want to divide the list into two sections—things that can be purchased in advance and perishables to be bought the day before the party.

The what-to-do-when list. This may seem like a time and motion plan;however, it will force you to be organized and will eliminate those last minute aggravations (turning the oven on, taking ice cream out of the freezer).

III. Party Time

There's no special formula for planning party activities. What you plan to do depends on the tastes and habits of your guests. Some adults will shun any type of game playing, preferring a social evening that revolves around conversation and meeting new people. Others are eager to participate in competitions.

Children react differently at each age level in party situations.

Four to six—they enjoy simple things—stuffed animals—a circus atmosphere.

Seven to nine—they enjoy making things—are imaginative—and love loot, favors, and prizes.

Ten to thirteen—they enjoy doing their own decorating, helping with food preparation, and playing games of skill that require physical dexterity.

The pages that follow offer many party situations for all ages. With each Cut-Up Cake we have recommended a special kind of party and some party activities. We hope these ideas will spark your imagination and that you will add your own personal touch and flair—creating parties that are in tune with your life style.

You don't have to limit party themes to those suggested. Interchange the games and party themes or try your own ideas. The cakes are all so versatile that you can mix and match the themes, activities, and ideas. A frowning Witch can wear a smile—the Umbrella can change colors. A touch of whimsy and assorted candies—that's all it takes to be your own creative decorator. If you don't have the exact candies listed for each recipe, be creative and substitute what you have on hand.

HAPPY DAY CAKE

- 2½ cups sifted Swans Down Cake Flour
- 3 teaspoons Calumet Baking Powder
- 1 teaspoon salt
- 1½ cups sugar
- ½ cup shortening (at room temperature)
- ¾ cup milk
- 1 teaspoon vanilla
- 2 eggs
- ¼ cup milk

Sift flour with baking powder, salt, and sugar.

Stir shortening just to soften. Add flour mixture, 3/4 cup milk, and the vanilla. Mix until all flour is moistened; then *beat 2 minutes* at medium speed of electric mixer or 300 vigorous strokes by hand, scraping bowl occasionally.

Add eggs and remaining 1/4 cup milk; *beat 1 minute* longer in mixer or 150 strokes by hand.

Pour batter into two 9-inch layer pans which have been lined on bottoms with waxpaper. Bake at 350° for 30-35 minutes, or until cake tester inserted into center comes out clean. Cool cakes in pans 10 minutes; then remove from pans and finish cooling on racks.

Alternate Baking Pans: This cake may also be baked in three 8-inch layer pans at 350° for 25 to 30 minutes, or in a 13 x 9-inch pan for 30 to 35 minutes.

MIX-EASY DEVIL'S FOOD CAKE

1¾ cups sifted Swans Down Cake Flour
1 teaspoon baking soda
¾ teaspoon salt
1⅓ cups sugar
½ cup butter or margarine
1 cup milk
1 teaspoon vanilla
2 eggs
3 squares Baker's Unsweetened
    Chocolate, melted

Sift flour with soda, salt, and sugar.

Stir butter to soften. Add flour mixture, milk, and vanilla. Mix until all flour is moistened; then *beat 2 minutes* at medium speed of electric mixer or 300 vigorous strokes by hand, scraping side of bowl occasionally.

Add eggs and chocolate. *Beat 1 minute* longer with mixer or 150 vigorous strokes by hand.

Pour batter into two 9-inch layer pans which have been lined on bottoms with wax paper. Bake at 350° for 30 to 35 minutes, or until cake tester inserted into center comes out clean. Cool cakes in pans 10 minutes; then remove from pans and cool thoroughly on racks.

Alternate Baking Pans: This cake may also be baked in a 13 x 9-inch pan for 40 minutes, in a 10-inch square pan for 45 minutes, or in two 9-inch square pans for 25 minutes.

SEVEN MINUTE FROSTING

(Makes 6¾ cups)

3 egg whites, unbeaten
2¼ cups sugar
⅛ teaspoon salt
½ cup water
1 tablespoon light corn syrup
1½ teaspoons vanilla

Combine egg whites, sugar, salt, water, and corn syrup in top of 2-quart double boiler. Beat about 1 minute, or until thoroughly mixed. Then place over boiling water and beat constantly with rotary beater (or at high speed of electric mixer) 7 minutes, or until frosting will stand in stiff peaks. (Stir frosting up from bottom and sides of pan occasionally with rubber scraper, spatula, or spoon.)

Remove from boiling water. For a very smooth and satiny frosting, pour at once into a large bowl for final beating. Then add vanilla and beat 1 minute, or until thick enough to spread.

FLUFFY SEVEN MINUTE FROSTING

(Makes 5⅓ cups)

            2 egg whites
        1½ cups sugar
            Dash of salt
        ½ cup water
            1 tablespoon light corn syrup
        1¼ teaspoons vanilla

Combine egg whites, sugar, salt, water, and corn syrup in top of double boiler. Beat about 1 minute or until thoroughly mixed. Then place over boiling water and beat constantly with rotary beater (or at high speed of electric mixer) 7 minutes, or until frosting will stand in stiff peaks, stirring frosting up from bottom and sides of pan occasionally with a rubber scraper, spatula, or spoon.

Remove from boiling water. For a very smooth and satiny frosting, pour at once into a large bowl for final beating. Then add vanilla and beat 1 minute, or until thick enough to spread.

BUTTER CREAM FROSTING

(Makes 2½ cups)

½ cup butter or margarine
⅛ teaspoon salt
1 pound (about 4½ cups) unsifted
   confectioners sugar
2 egg yolks, unbeaten*
1 teaspoon vanilla
2 tablespoons (about) milk

*Or use 1 whole egg.

Cream butter until soft. Add salt and part of sugar gradually, blending after each addition. Then add egg yolks and vanilla; blend well. Add remaining sugar, alternately with milk, until of right consistency to spread, beating after each addition until smooth.

FOUR MINUTE FROSTING

(Makes 2 cups)

1 egg white
¾ cup sugar
Dash of salt
3 tablespoons water
1 teaspoon light corn syrup
½ teaspoon vanilla

Combine egg white, sugar, salt, water, and corn syrup in top of small double boiler or in small bowl. Beat with electric mixer or rotary beater until thoroughly mixed—about 1 minute. Place over boiling water and beat constantly at high speed of electric mixer (or with rotary beater) until frosting stands in stiff peaks—about 4 minutes, stirring frosting up from bottom and sides of pan occasionally with rubber scraper, spatula, or spoon.

Remove from boiling water. For a very smooth and satiny frosting, pour at once into a large bowl for final beating. Add vanilla and beat until thick enough to spread—about 1 minute.

A Few Friendly Tips . . .

CHOCOLATE

To Melt Chocolate

There are favorite ways to melt chocolate. Whatever method you use, remember that chocolate scorches easily and that melted semi-sweet and sweet chocolates tend to hold their shape until stirred.

Over hot water: Place chocolate in top of double boiler. Heat over hot water 10 to 12 minutes. Or use a custard cup or saucepan set in a pan of water. If you prefer, melt unsweetened squares wrapped with folded ends up. Then carefully lift and scrape chocolate off the wrappers.

In liquid: In some recipes, the chocolate may be melted with the shortening or in the milk or water over very low direct heat, stirring constantly. If necessary, beat until thoroughly blended and smooth.

In Oven: While oven preheats or if it has been turned off but is still warm, set the wrapped or unwrapped squares on a pan or piece of foil in the oven until melted. Of course, oven should not be too hot, nor should chocolate be left in oven too long.

Over very low direct heat: Unwrap the chocolate and place in a small saucepan over *very low* heat. Stir constantly until chocolate melts. Or set over a pilot light or on an asbestos mat over very low heat and stir chocolate occasionally. Remove from heat as soon as the chocolate melts.

To Store Chocolate

Keep chocolate in a reasonably cool place —below 75° F. if possible. At very high temperatures, the cocoa butter melts into the wrapper and the chocolate loses some of its fine flavor. But if chocolate grays in color, cocoa butter has merely risen to top and neither flavor nor quality is impaired.

COCONUT

To store coconut

An unopened package of Baker's Coconut may be kept on your kitchen shelf. However, after opening the package, the coconut will remain moist and tasty longer if stored in the refrigerator in the tightly reclosed package or a covered container.

TINTED COCONUT

½ teaspoon milk or water
Few drops food coloring
1⅓ cups (3½ oz.) Baker's Angel
Flake Coconut

Mix milk and food coloring in a bowl. Add coconut and toss with a fork until coconut is evenly tinted.

Or place coconut in a glass jar, filling jar not more than half full. Mix food coloring and milk; sprinkle over coconut. Cover jar and shake vigorously until evenly tinted.

TOASTED COCONUT
Baker's Angel Flake Coconut

Thinly spread coconut in shallow baking pan. Toast in a 350° oven for 7 to 12 minutes, or until lightly browned. Stir coconut or shake pan often to toast evenly.

CHOCOLATE-COATED COCONUT

1   package (4 oz.) Baker's German's
        Sweet Chocolate, broken in pieces*
1⅓ cups (about) Baker's Angel Flake
        Coconut, toasted or plain

*Or use 2 squares Baker's
    Semi-Sweet Chocolate.

Heat chocolate in small saucepan over low heat until partly melted. Remove from heat; stir rapidly until entirely melted. Add coconut and mix well. Spread on baking sheet, separating flakes of coconut with a fork. Chill until chocolate is set. Store in a tightly covered jar. Serve as topping on frosted cake, ice cream, or pudding. Makes about 2 cups.

Note: Recipe may be halved.

AIRPLANE

Destination Monte Carlo!!

Join the Jet Set and pretend to spend an evening at Monte Carlo. Tables are clear for take-off and the Airplane Cut-Up is the point of departure.

Invitations can be made from an old deck of cards. Staple an itinerary sheet to each card giving time, place, and a brief description of what's in store.

Each guest is given an envelope of play money. Set up tables for cards, roulette, dice, and borrow a pinball machine from the children.

Post house game rules at each table and ask guests to take turns at being dealer, banker, and wheel spinner. Have prize for the biggest winner and a consolation prize for the biggest loser. Serve a midnight buffet of assorted breads, cheeses, and cold cuts.

WHAT YOU WILL NEED

1 baked 9-inch square
   cake,* cooled
5⅓ cups Seven Minute
   Frosting
2 cups Baker's Angel
   Flake Coconut

Yellow food coloring
Large black gumdrops
Small red candy
   coated chocolate
   candies
Small green gumdrops

*Use 3 cups batter baked at 350° for about
25 minutes. Remaining batter may be used
to bake 12 to 15 medium cupcakes.

1 Cut cake as shown
in diagram. Shaded
pieces are not used.
Tint 1/2 cup coconut
yellow.

cut in eight
equal sections

2 Arrange cake,
using frosting to
hold pieces
together. Pieces
E, F, and **G** are
placed on cake cut
side down. Frost
entire cake,
rounding corners
for better
appearance.

3 Sprinkle with coconut and decorate with candy as shown.

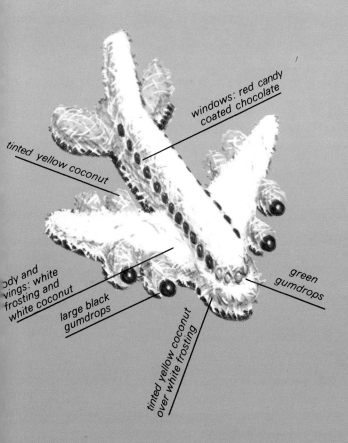

windows: red candy coated chocolate

tinted yellow coconut

body and wings: white frosting and white coconut

large black gumdrops

tinted yellow coconut over white frosting

green gumdrops

ANGEL

The Little Angel Cut-Up wings in to say Happy Birthday to your special little angel. You can set a perfectly heavenly scene for all the sprightly little ones at this fanciful party.

For each child cut out a pair of angel wings. Use white construction paper with spots of glued-on sparkles or glitter. Fold back a 2-inch margin along straight edge and punch holes at top and bottom. Use ribbon or yarn to tie on wings.

Make halos by cutting headbands out of yellow construction paper. Attach a pipe cleaner that is topped with a small balloon. Secure to children's heads with bobby pins. Cover party table with pastel nylon net. Sprinkle with multi-colored stick-on stars. For an angel band, be ready with little toy musical instruments such as flutes, horns, banjos, etc.

WHAT YOU WILL NEED

1 baked 13 x 9-inch cake, cooled
5⅓ cups Seven Minute Frosting
1⅓ cups (about) Baker's Angel Flake Coconut

Red and yellow food coloring
Red gumdrop
Yellow gumdrops
Chocolate sprinkles
Silver dragées
Red sugar sprinkles

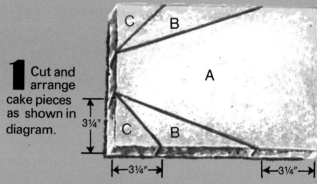

1 Cut and arrange cake pieces as shown in diagram.

3¼"

3¼"

3¼"

C B A

C B

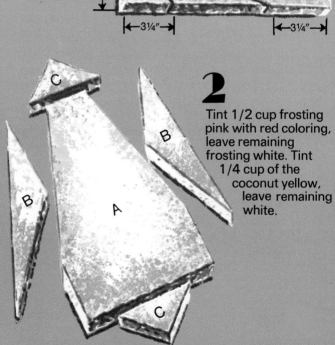

2 Tint 1/2 cup frosting pink with red coloring, leave remaining frosting white. Tint 1/4 cup of the coconut yellow, leave remaining white.

3 Use white frosting to hold cake pieces in place. Make angel's face with pink frosting as shown in diagram. Frost remaining cake with white frosting. Use yellow coconut for angel's hair. Sprinkle white coconut over white frosting. Use cut red gumdrop for mouth and nose. Place other candies as shown.

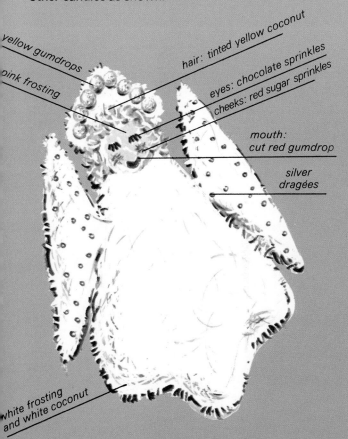

yellow gumdrops

pink frosting

hair: tinted yellow coconut

eyes: chocolate sprinkles

cheeks: red sugar sprinkles

mouth:
cut red gumdrop

silver
dragées

white frosting
and white coconut

THE BEAUTIFUL BALLOON

Arrival Time!

Phineas Fogg and Jules Verne would approve of drifting in from out of the blue to see this Beautiful Balloon Cut-Up—landing right on target for a Welcome Home Party. Secure all holds and clear the way for a super buffet.

Plan an international menu. Ask friends to bring a foreign flavored specialty suggesting that it be appetizer, main dish, salad, or vegetable accompaniment.

Decorate with travel posters, maps, and charts. Set aside time for showing travel slides—yours, the honor guests, or a composite of four or five of everyone's favorites.

Ask everyone to come in costume representing some far off place. Award prizes for most authentic, funniest, and most original outfit.

WHAT YOU WILL NEED

- 1 baked 8-inch round cake layer, cooled
- 1 baked 9-inch round cake layer, cooled
- 5⅓ cups Seven Minute Frosting
- 2⅔ cups (about) Baker's Angel Flake Coconut

Red, green, and yellow food coloring
Black licorice laces
Pastel candies
Small dolls (optional)

1 The 9-inch cake layer forms the balloon. Cut 8-inch layer to form pieces **A** and **B**. Split piece **A** through center to make two thin identical pieces.

C — 9″ dia.

A

B — 8″ dia.

2½″ split to make 2 layers

C

2 Position cakes on large tray. Place pieces **A** on top of **B**, using frosting to secure, contour, and cover cake. Tint 1/2 cup coconut red, 1/2 cup green, and 1-1/3 cups yellow. Leave remaining coconut untinted. Make stripes on balloon with coconut as shown.

A

A

B

3 Cover basket completely with yellow-tinted coconut. Position dolls. Arrange licorice and candies as shown.

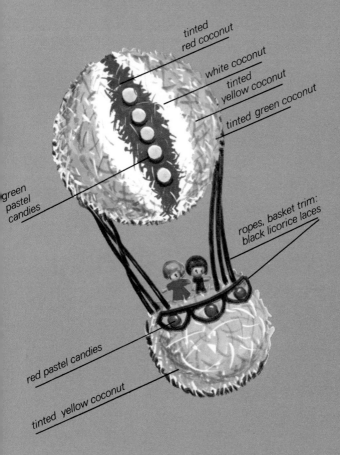

tinted red coconut

white coconut

tinted yellow coconut

tinted green coconut

green pastel candies

ropes, basket trim: black licorice laces

red pastel candies

tinted yellow coconut

BUTTERFLY

How sweet it is to be sixteen, when the hearts of young girls are all aflutter. Just as pretty and graceful as that age can be is the Butterfly Cut-Up—a light and airy center-piece to mark the birthday occasion.

Plan a dinner dance for eight couples. Set up four cardtables that are covered to the floor with pastel sheets. Pin on butterfly cut-outs to form an attractive scalloped hem. Serve food from the buffet, yet ask guests to be seated at little tables, and after each course, everyone must change seats so that each sits opposite a different person.

Suggest that each guest bring a favorite record. Let guests select a disc jockey time slot from a hat. During that time (8:00 to 8:15) that person is responsible for choosing the platter and providing the chatter.

WHAT YOU WILL NEED

1 baked 13 x 9-inch cake, cooled
5⅓ cups Seven Minute Frosting, tinted pale yellow
1⅓ cups (about) Baker's Angel Flake Coconut

Yellow food coloring
Large and small gumdrops
Black licorice sticks
Black licorice laces

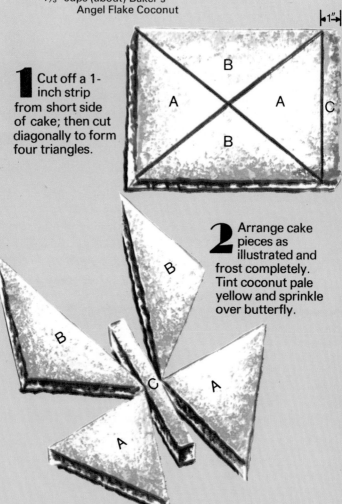

1 Cut off a 1-inch strip from short side of cake; then cut diagonally to form four triangles.

2 Arrange cake pieces as illustrated and frost completely. Tint coconut pale yellow and sprinkle over butterfly.

3 Slice gumdrops and licorice and arrange candies on wings and body as shown. Use licorice laces for curled antennas.

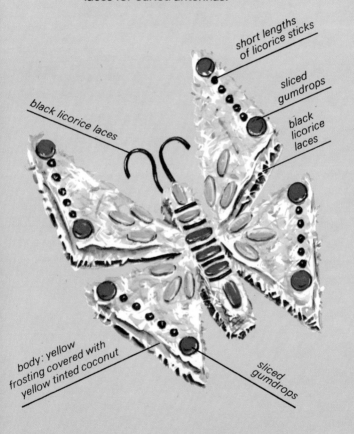

short lengths of licorice sticks

sliced gumdrops

black licorice laces

black licorice laces

body: yellow frosting covered with yellow tinted coconut

sliced gumdrops

CABIN CRUISER

Ship—Ahoy!

It's Bon Voyage time. Off for a pleasure cruise, fishing trip, or seaman's adventure, the Cabin Cruiser Cut-Up Cake bids smooth sailing all the way.

All types of water-sports equipment can be used for decorating—such as snorkle masks, fins, water skis, and fishing poles. Display charts and safety rules and string pennants at the entrance.

The menu message is food from the sea. For simple fare, mugs of chowder with assorted crackers and cheese—or fishburgers or cone-shaped paper containers with fish and chips. For a buffet or sit-down dinner, prepare a favorite fish casserole or a whole baked or poached fish.

WHAT YOU WILL NEED

1 baked 13 x 9-inch cake, cooled
5⅓ cups Seven Minute Frosting
2⅔ cups (about) Baker's Angel Flake Coconut
Blue food coloring

7 ring-shaped hard candies
3 large orange gumdrops
1 doughnut-shaped gumdrop
Black licorice laces
Small United States Flag

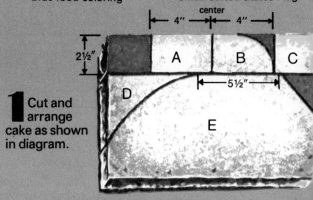

1 Cut and arrange cake as shown in diagram.

2 Use frosting to hold cake pieces together, then, cover entire cake with remaining frosting. Tint 1-1/2 cups of coconut blue.

3 Decorate with coconut and candies as illustrated. To flatten gumdrops for windows, cut large gumdrops in half and flatten with rolling pin; then pull or cut to correct shape.

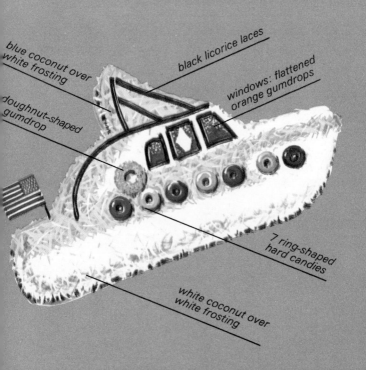

blue coconut over white frosting

black licorice laces

doughnut-shaped gumdrop

windows: flattened orange gumdrops

7 ring-shaped hard candies

white coconut over white frosting

CANNONBALL EXPRESS

ALL ABOARD! The Cannonball Express is a direct route for little passengers to a Happy Birthday Party. Ring the bell and blow the whistle to signal it's time for full speed ahead to fun and games.

Send invitations that look like railroad timetables. Display maps on walls and indicate with marking pen cities to be visited. Give children play money and let them purchase tickets from a "conductor" helper to selected destination.

Refreshments can be served train snack-bar style with wrapped sandwiches, milk cartons and straws, or paper cups of soft drinks.

Check local library for films on railroads. Precede the party with a visit to a nearby museum that offers an antique model train exhibit.

WHAT YOU WILL NEED

1   baked 13 x 9-inch
    cake, cooled
5⅓ cups Seven Minute
    Frosting
1⅓ cups (about) Baker's
    Angel Flake Coconut
    Red food coloring

2   orange lollipops
3   large marshmallows
3   large yellow gumdrops
    Black licorice laces
    Black ribbon licorice

1 Cut cake as shown in diagram. Arrange on a large tray using frosting to hold pieces together.

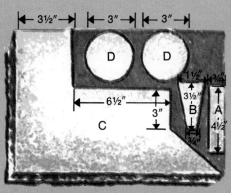

2 Spread cake with frosting, making corners sharp for better looks. Tint coconut red, and sprinkle on as illustrated.

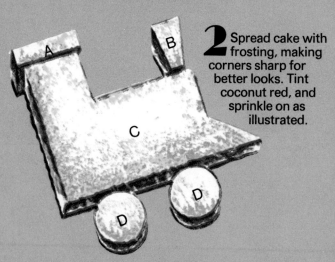

3 Decorate with marsh-mallows, candy, and licorice as shown.

marshmallows

cab, wheels grill: white frosting

yellow gumdrops

black licorice laces

black licorice laces

tinted red coconut

black ribbon licorice

wheel centers: orange lollipops

CHRISTMAS TREE

A caroling we will go. Everyone joins in heralding the joys of Christmas time. Wind-up the song fest by inviting carolers in to light the Christmas Tree Cut-Up Cake and share your warm hospitality.

Decide upon a time and meeting place. Choose one member of the group to be responsible for selecting where the singing will take place.

Make copies of the words to the carols that will be sung. Suggest that carolers bring flashlights and wear something bright for a nighttime session. A string of jingle bells adds to the merriment.

Conclude with hot mugs of punch or cider and the Christmas Tree Cut-Up Cake.

WHAT YOU WILL NEED

- 1 baked 9-inch square cake,* cooled
- 5⅓ cups Seven Minute Frosting, tinted pale green
- 1½ cups Baker's Angel Flake Coconut
- ½ cup Chocolate-Coated Coconut
- Green food coloring
- Large and small silver dragées
- Red ball candies
- Red candles
- Large black gumdrop

1 Cut cake into two rectangles. Then cut each rectangle as shown in diagram. Arrange cake using frosting to hold pieces together.

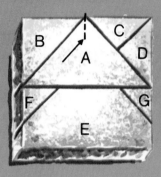

2 Frost entire cake. Sprinkle Chocolate-Coated Coconut over trunk. Tint coconut green and sprinkle over rest of cake.

For 9-inch square cake, bake *all* of prepared cake mix batter in a greased, floured 9-inch square pan at 325° for 50 to 55 minutes, or until cake tests done.

3 Flatten a large black gumdrop; cut into star shape; stud thickly with silver dragées for tree-top ornament. Finish decorating with dragées, candies, and candles.

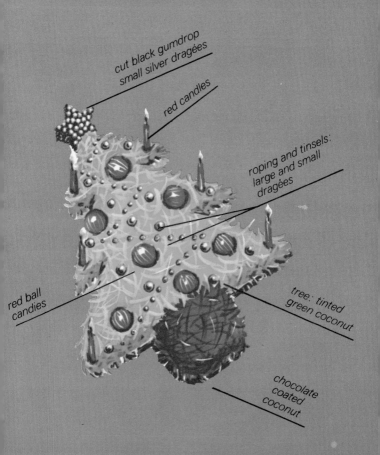

cut black gumdrop small silver dragées

red candles

roping and tinsels; large and small dragées

tree: tinted green coconut

red ball candies

chocolate coated coconut

CLOWN

It's Showtime!

Raise the footlights, pull back the curtains —
set the stage for a Do-Your-Own-Thing Teen
Party. Jovial jokers one and all take a clue
from the Clown Cut-Up for some happy
hilarity.

Begin with a box of old clothes; include
hats, wigs, mop heads, odds and ends of
materials. Set up a table with theatrical
makeup and mirror. (Don't forget to provide
an ample supply of cleansing tissues and
cold cream for easy removal of makeup.)

Brown paper bags rolled at the top and
twisted at the bottom make fun hats. Provide
crayons, stick-ons, pieces of costume jewelry
and watch the wild results.

Plan a joke-telling contest or a competition
awarding a prize to the person who can
make the most people laugh — in the shortest
period of time. Another prize goes to the
person who manages not to crack a smile
in a given time period (no touching or
tickling allowed).

WHAT YOU WILL NEED

- 1 baked 8-inch round cake layer, cooled
- 1 baked 8-inch square cake layer, cooled
- 5⅓ cups Seven Minute Frosting
- 2 cups Baker's Angel Flake Coconut

Green, red, yellow, and blue food coloring
- 2 large black gumdrops
- 1 large red gumdrop
- 7 small red gumdrops
- 1 large marshmallow
  Miniature marshmallows
  Black licorice laces
- 2 small white candies

1 Cut a 1-inch wide piece from round cake. Cut this piece in half (**A**). Follow diagram in cutting the square cake. Assemble clown, inverting piece **E**, and using frosting to hold pieces together. Cover completely with frosting.

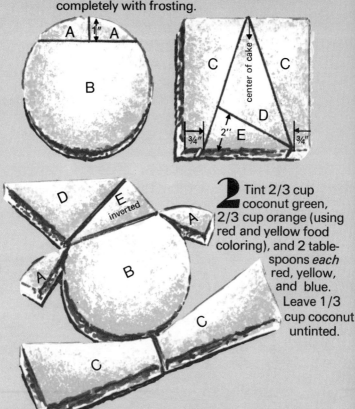

2 Tint 2/3 cup coconut green, 2/3 cup orange (using red and yellow food coloring), and 2 tablespoons *each* red, yellow, and blue. Leave 1/3 cup coconut untinted.

3 Sprinkle untinted coconut on sides of bow. Use tinted red, blue, and yellow coconut for polka dots. Finish decorating cake with green-and orange-tinted coconut. Make eyes from flattened and cut large black gumdrops. Add marshmallows, licorice, and candy as shown.

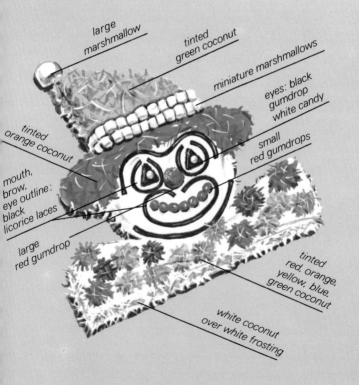

large marshmallow

tinted green coconut

miniature marshmallows

eyes: black gumdrop white candy

tinted orange coconut

small red gumdrops

mouth, brow, eye outline: black licorice laces

large red gumdrop

tinted red, orange, yellow, blue, green coconut

white coconut over white frosting

CUDDLY BUNNY

Cuddly Bunny Cut-Up leads the parade in extending Easter greetings. Decked out in all his finery, he looks particularly fashionable at an Easter afternoon Tea Party.

Send egg-shaped invitations cut out of construction paper and trimmed with bits of rick-rack, yarn, and glitter.

Ask guests to wear a favorite Easter bonnet and award a prize for the prettiest, funniest, and most original.

Use decorated baskets to hold candy, nuts, napkins, and silverware.

Fill a jar with a counted number of jelly beans. Let each guest sign in and write down the number of candies he thinks the jar contains. Have the correct number in a sealed envelope. At the appropriate time open the envelope and award a toy rabbit to the person who comes the closest to the right count.

WHAT YOU WILL NEED

2 baked 9-inch round
    cake layers, cooled
5⅓ cups Seven Minute
    Frosting
2⅔ cups (about) Baker's
    Angel Flake Coconut

Red food coloring
2 black licorice laces
1 red, 1 pink, 2 black
    jelly beans
Red bow

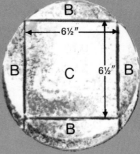

1 Cut round edges off one layer as shown, making a 6-inch square. Edges become ears. Cut ring 1-1/2 inches wide around second layer; divide into 8 equal pieces for the paws.

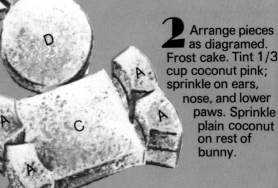

2 Arrange pieces as diagramed. Frost cake. Tint 1/3 cup coconut pink; sprinkle on ears, nose, and lower paws. Sprinkle plain coconut on rest of bunny.

3 Decorate with licorice, jelly beans, red bow.

ears:
pink coconut

pink jelly bean

red bow

eyes: black
jelly bean

red jelly bean

feet:
pink
coconut

brows, mouth,
paws: black
licorice laces

white coconut
over white frosting

DAISY

Daisies Do Tell — when they turn up at a party. The Daisy Cut-Up sets a bright and sunny mood for a Happy Birthday. Especially appropriate in April, the month for daisies and diamonds.

Plan a dessert and coffee party. Keep the color scheme yellow, white, and green. Use your favorite candelabra or taper candles set in florists clay and covered with fresh green lemon leaves or fern.

Ask guests to bring a small gift following the daisy theme. Some suggestions might include note paper, paper napkins, jewelry, or a plant. Or, suggest that the talented members of the group make something — a miniature painting, crochet-edged handkerchief, decorated coffee mug, or a bit of imaginative stitchery.

WHAT YOU WILL NEED

2 baked 9-inch round
   cake layers, cooled
8 cups Seven Minute
   Frosting
2⅔ cups (about) Baker's
   Angel Flake Coconut

Green food coloring
1 can (8¾ oz.) crushed
   pineapple, drained

1 Cut cakes as shown in diagram. Arrange cake using frosting to hold pieces in place.

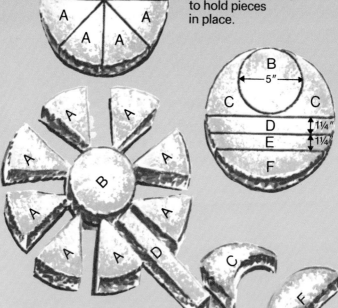

2 Tint 1/2 cup of the coconut green. Frost entire cake. Sprinkle green coconut on stem and leaves. Sprinkle remaining coconut on petals *only*.

3 Arrange pineapple in center of daisy as illustrated.

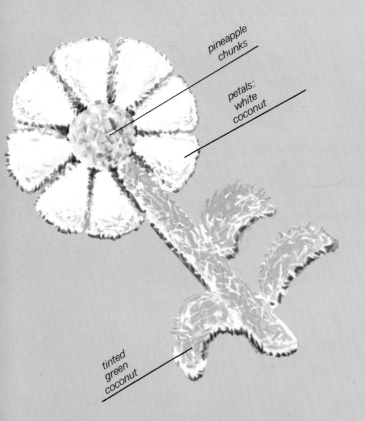

pineapple chunks

petals: white coconut

tinted green coconut

EASY BUNNY

HOKUS...POKUS...DOMINOKUS...

Magicians can turn a Birthday Party for children into a wide-eyed time of wonderment. And as a perennial partner to all magicians, Easy Bunny Cut-Up can be the final treat.

Check with local high schools or junior highs for a young amateur magician or check with little theater groups who may be able to recommend a professional.

A visit to a magic and novelty store will reveal a number of inexpensive little favors that can be wrapped and placed in a large sack or pillow-case labeled "Bag of Tricks." Let each child reach in for his own special take home magic.

WHAT YOU WILL NEED

2 baked 9-inch round
   cake layers, cooled
5⅓ cups Seven Minute
   Frosting
1⅓ cups (about) Baker's
   Angel Flake Coconut

Red food coloring
Small pastel-colored
   gumdrops
Red and black
   licorice laces

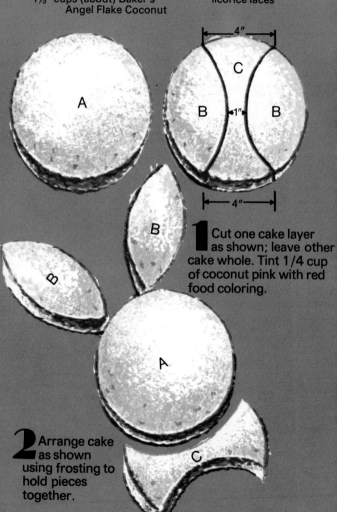

1 Cut one cake layer as shown; leave other cake whole. Tint 1/4 cup of coconut pink with red food coloring.

2 Arrange cake as shown using frosting to hold pieces together.

3 Frost entire cake. Sprinkle with coconut and decorate with licorice and gum-drops as shown.

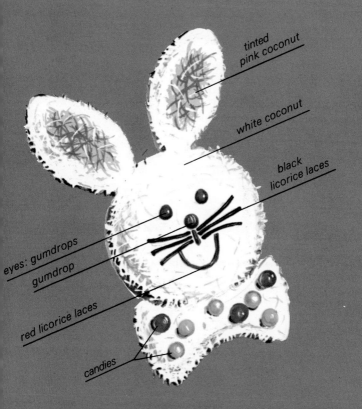

tinted pink coconut

white coconut

black licorice laces

eyes: gumdrops

gumdrop

red licorice laces

candies

FLOWER CART

Come to my party

The Flower Cart Cut-Up Cake is ready to bloom for a Garden Party any time of year. And should your garden be out of season, turn a sunny room into a gazebo for the occasion.

For invitations, trace a silhouette of your hand on single sheets of writing paper, and be sure to color the thumb green.

Instead of place cards, use packages of seeds that can double as gifts for guests to keep. To carry out the party theme, use clean garden equipment in novel ways. Water containers can be used as pitchers for punch, redwood tubs lined with foil make fine ice buckets, and a decorated wheel barrel can hold large bowls of salads. For entertainment, invite the garden editor of the local paper or ask a talented friend or local florist to give hints on flower arranging.

Ask each guest to bring a small inexpensive potted plant, attach numbers to each, and have a drawing for another take home memento.

DAISY

WHAT YOU WILL NEED

1 baked 13 x 9-inch cake, cooled
5⅓ cups Seven Minute Frosting
2 cups Baker's Angel Flake Coconut
Red and yellow food coloring
2 red candy sticks (about 4½ inches long)
Large green and yellow gumdrops

Small gumdrops
Green gumdrops
Small jelly beans
Red licorice laces
Black rope licorice
Wooden picks

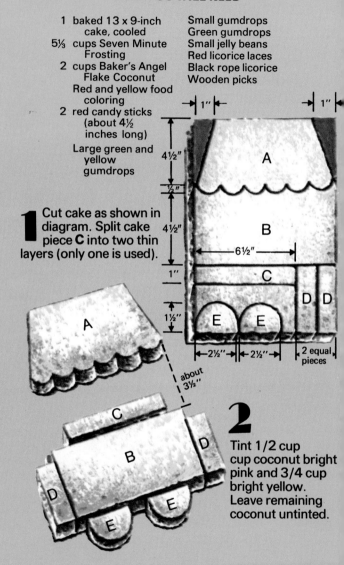

1 Cut cake as shown in diagram. Split cake piece **C** into two thin layers (only one is used).

1" 1"

4½"
½"
4½"
6½"
1"
1½"

A
B
C
D D
E E

2½" 2½"
2 equal pieces

about 3½"

2 Tint 1/2 cup cup coconut bright pink and 3/4 cup bright yellow. Leave remaining coconut untinted.

3 Arrange cake as shown, using frosting to hold pieces together. Frost cake completely. Pat on coconut as shown. Arrange candy flowers and leaves shaped from green gumdrops, using wooden picks to hold in place.

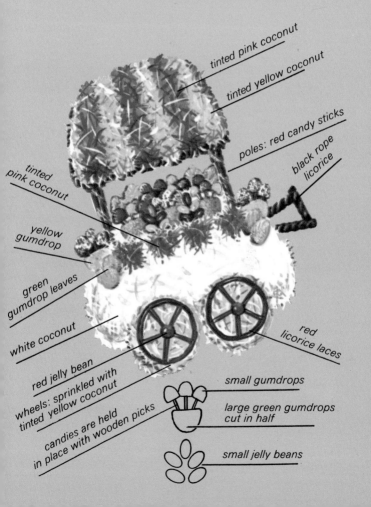

tinted pink coconut

tinted yellow coconut

poles: red candy sticks

black rope licorice

tinted pink coconut

yellow gumdrop

green gumdrop leaves

white coconut

red licorice laces

red jelly bean

wheels: sprinkled with tinted yellow coconut

candies are held in place with wooden picks

small gumdrops

large green gumdrops cut in half

small jelly beans

HAPPY HOUSE

The Doors are open—everything is set for a "join in the fun" Housewarming. Since the house is what it's all about and what everyone wants to see—The Happy House Cut-Up Cake gets star billing.

Send invitations that reflect your decorating scheme... leftover pieces of wallpaper or plain white cards with splashes of your colors. If inviting a very large crowd, you might want to stagger arrival times.

Have a large box of leftover materials such as pieces of wood, slate, formica, carpeting, fabric and wallpaper. Stand up a large canvas or piece of burlap on a stretcher. Let each guest pick something and glue or staple it to the base for a Kooky Collage. Felt tip marking pens can be used for sketches or messages.

Refreshments can be napkin-wrapped, man-sized sandwiches. (No plates required.) For dessert, mugs of coffee and the cake.

WHAT YOU WILL NEED

2 baked 8-inch square
  cakes, cooled
5⅓ cups Seven Minute
  Frosting
2 cups Baker's Angel
  Flake Coconut
Red food coloring
Black licorice laces

Chocolate rolls
Baker's Semi-Sweet
  Chocolate Chips
Green gumdrops
Orange gumdrop rolls
Yellow ring-shaped
  hard candies
Marshmallows

1 Cut one cake into two equal halves. Cut the other into 4 triangles (only 3 are used).

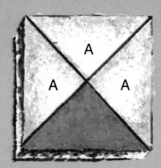

center of cake

2 Spread frosting between pieces and put together in shape of house as shown. Set triangles back from front, leaving base clear for balcony. Finish frosting.

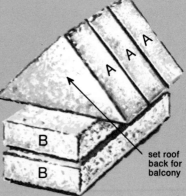

set roof
back for
balcony

3 Pat about 1 cup coconut around sides of house. Thatch roof with more coconut, tinted red. Decorate with candy as shown.

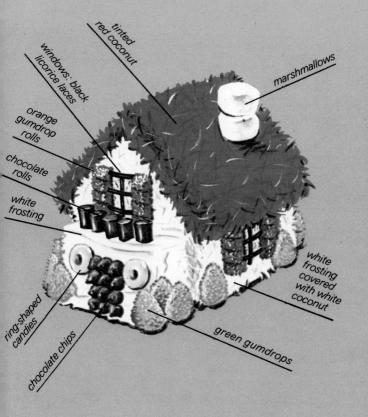

tinted red coconut

windows: black licorice laces

orange gumdrop rolls

chocolate rolls

white frosting

marshmallows

white frosting covered with white coconut

ring-shaped candies

chocolate chips

green gumdrops

A PAIR OF HEARTS

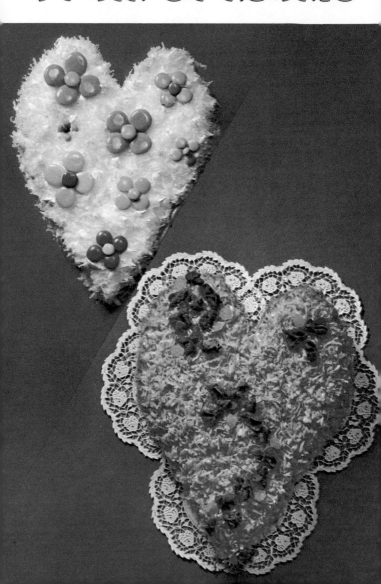

A pair of hearts that speak of love—one is as delicate as an old-fashioned Valentine—the other is cheerful, gay, and slightly mod. Either one can help celebrate an Anniversary in a loving way.

Key the party to the year being celebrated —first, paper; second, cotton; third, leather; fourth, fruits and flowers. When the couple shares a favorite hobby, or is enthusiastic about some particular sport, use that interest as the party theme.

Instead of actual gifts let each invited couple present an I.O.U. for some special favor to be collected within the coming year... an evening of baby-sitting, a homemade gourmet specialty, a mowed lawn, help with a home project, etc.

Top off the party with a champagne or wine punch and the cake.

WHAT YOU WILL NEED FOR EACH CAKE

2 baked 8-inch round
   cake layers, cooled
5⅓ cups Seven Minute
   Frosting
1⅓ cups (about) Baker's
   Angel Flake Coconut
Pastel candies, or
   candied violets and
   green gumdrops

1 For *each* cake, spread frosting between layers. Cut cake pieces as shown in diagram.

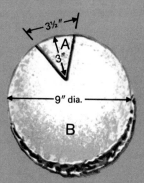

2 Arrange cake as diagramed, holding pieces together and smoothing out heart shape with frosting. For Victorian heart, tint frosting and coconut pink.

3 Spread remaining frosting over cake; then sprinkle with coconut. Decorate with candies using mints for modern white heart and candied violets and green gumdrops for the Victorian heart.

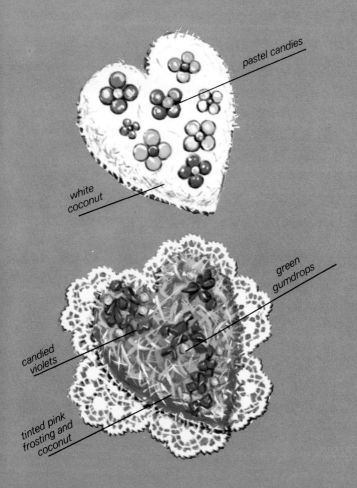

pastel candies

white coconut

green gumdrops

candied violets

tinted pink frosting and coconut

THE PERFECT DOLL

No doubt about the new arrival —
that expected baby is bound to be a
doll. Girl or boy — or one of each
— the Perfect Doll Cut-Up Cake fits
right into the Baby Shower celebration.

Plan a Kaffeeklatsch scheduled at the
coffee hour. For invitations, buy an inexpensive baby book. Tear out pages and use
these for writing invitations.

When the guests arrive, distribute pencils
and a supply of pink and blue paper folded in
half. Ask each guest to write a favorite "helpful
hint" on baby care, a favorite nursery rhyme,
or an original limerick. Bind the pages
together with pink and blue yarn to
make a party souvenir scrapbook for
the honored mother-to-be. For the
outside cover, use children's
wallpaper, colorful vinyl material,
or construction paper with a
drawing of the perfect doll.
Include all the guests'
signatures inside.

WHAT YOU WILL NEED

1 baked 8-inch round cake layer, cooled
1 baked 8-inch square cake layer, cooled
5⅓ cups Seven Minute Frosting
1½ cups Baker's Angel Flake Coconut

Red, blue, and yellow food coloring
Pastel candies
Black and red gumdrops
Black licorice laces
Red licorice twists
White mint patties

1 Cut out cake pieces as shown. If making a girl doll, use pieces **A** for the legs—if a boy doll, use pieces **C** for the legs.

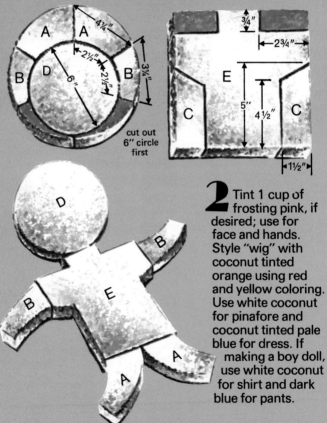

2 Tint 1 cup of frosting pink, if desired; use for face and hands. Style "wig" with coconut tinted orange using red and yellow coloring. Use white coconut for pinafore and coconut tinted pale blue for dress. If making a boy doll, use white coconut for shirt and dark blue for pants.

3

Flatten and cut large black and red gumdrops into shapes shown for eyes, nose, and mouth. Finish decorating with licorice laces, white mint patties, twists and candies.

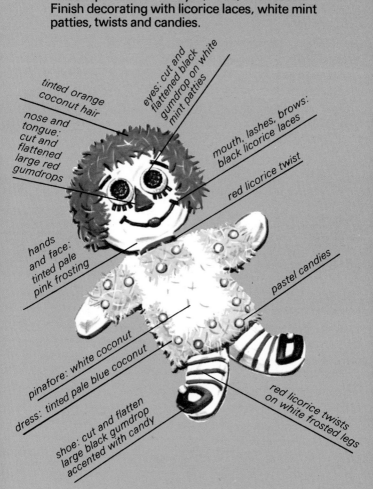

tinted orange coconut hair

eyes: cut and flattened black gumdrop on white mint patties

nose and tongue: cut and flattened large red gumdrops

mouth, lashes, brows: black licorice laces

red licorice twist

hands and face: tinted pale pink frosting

pastel candies

pinafore: white coconut

dress: tinted pale blue coconut

shoe: cut and flatten large black gumdrop accented with candy

red licorice twists on white frosted legs

PERKY TURKEY

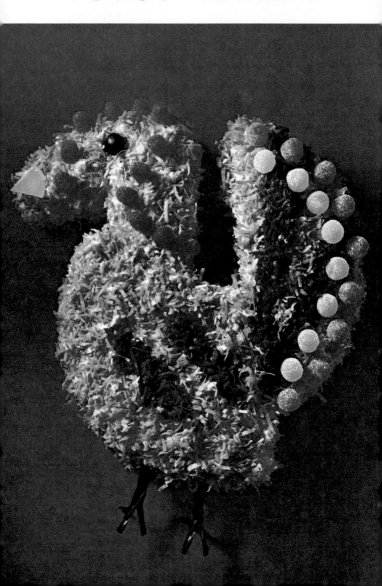

Perky Turkey Cut-Up wins rave reviews for a long run at holiday tables! This unruffled big bird is just right for carving at leisure during large gatherings, when adults get together for an evening of square dancing and country-style fun.

Hire a professional caller or let someone in your group do the calling. Old time records are fun for all — young and old alike.

Decorations are straight from nature's best — bales of hay, buckets or baskets filled with fresh fruit, and colorful bandanas that serve as napkins as well as a take-home souvenir. Let guests come in dungarees.

Award straw hats or corn cob pipes to best dancers or most energetic participants.

WHAT YOU WILL NEED

2 baked 9-inch round
    cake layers, cooled
5⅓ cups Seven Minute
    Frosting, tinted
    pale orange
1⅓ cups (about) Baker's
    Angel Flake Coconut,
    toasted

½ cup Chocolate-Coated
    Coconut
    Black licorice twists
    Orange, yellow, and
    red gumdrops
1 large yellow gumdrop
1 black licorice candy

1 Spread one cake layer with frosting.
Top with second layer. Cut and
arrange stacked layers on
serving platter as
diagramed, using
frosting to hold
pieces in place.

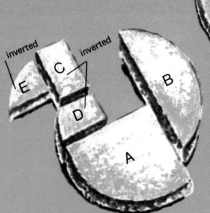

2 Finish frosting.
Cover thickly
with toasted cocon
making feathers wi
Chocolate-Coated
Coconut.

3 Flatten and cut large yellow gumdrop for beak. Finish decorating with licorice and candy as shown.

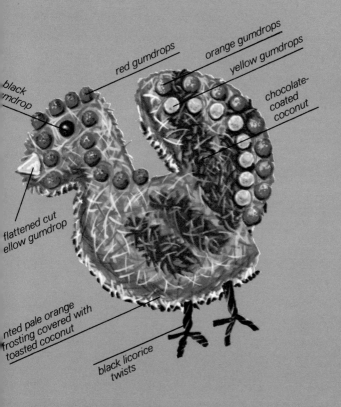

black gumdrop

red gumdrops

orange gumdrops

yellow gumdrops

chocolate-coated coconut

flattened cut yellow gumdrop

nted pale orange frosting covered with toasted coconut

black licorice twists

RACER

V–A–R–O–O–O–O–O–M !

Get things off to a fast start. Begin a birthday party for little car buffs with a giant roar. Surprise them with this Racer Cut-Up, and rev up for a few hours of action.

In good weather some outdoor races are fun and work off a bit of energy. Let each boy wear a different colored arm band or pin on numbers for the competition. A toy model car could be awarded the winner.

As an indoor game, set aside an area as a track with obstacles (throw pillows, balloons, empty paper cartons). Let the children study the track, then one by one blindfolded and twisted around, see who comes closest to staying on course.

WHAT YOU WILL NEED

- 1 baked 13 x 9-inch cake, cooled
- 5⅓ cups Seven Minute Frosting
- 1⅓ cups (about) Baker's Angel Flake Coconut Green and yellow food coloring

- 2 large nonpareils
- 2 chocolate kisses Black licorice twists
- 1 large orange gumdrop Chocolate sprinkles Doll race car driver (optional)

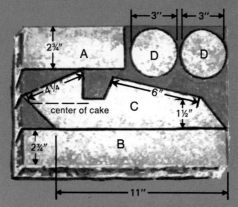

1 Cut two 3-inch circles (the wheels) from cake first; then, cut remaining cake as shown. Assemble cake, except for wheels, on a large tray.

2 Tint half of coconut light green and half yellow Spread cake, minus wheels, with frosting. Cover car and track with coconut as illustrated.

3 Frost wheels, roll through chocolate sprinkles; add hub caps of large nonpareils; and set in place. Cut number from rolled gumdrop. Decorate with licorice and chocolate kisses as shown.

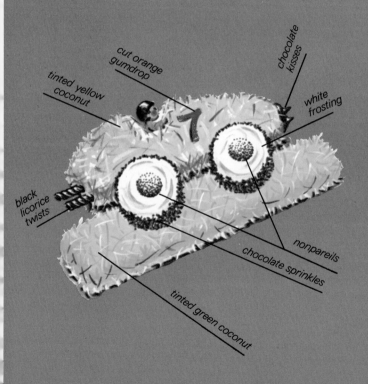

cut orange gumdrop

chocolate kisses

tinted yellow coconut

white frosting

black licorice twists

nonpareils

chocolate sprinkles

tinted green coconut

SAILBOAT

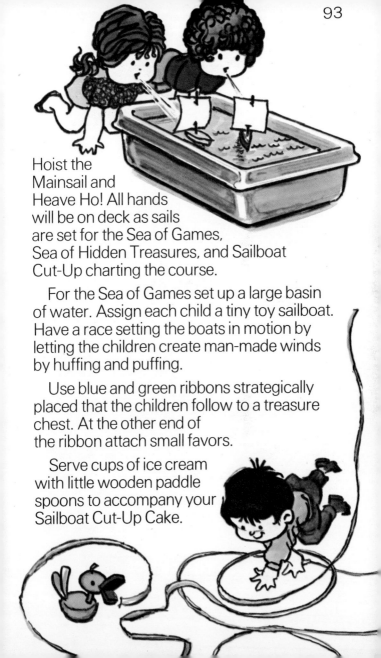

Hoist the
Mainsail and
Heave Ho! All hands
will be on deck as sails
are set for the Sea of Games,
Sea of Hidden Treasures, and Sailboat
Cut-Up charting the course.

For the Sea of Games set up a large basin
of water. Assign each child a tiny toy sailboat.
Have a race setting the boats in motion by
letting the children create man-made winds
by huffing and puffing.

Use blue and green ribbons strategically
placed that the children follow to a treasure
chest. At the other end of
the ribbon attach small favors.

Serve cups of ice cream
with little wooden paddle
spoons to accompany your
Sailboat Cut-Up Cake.

WHAT YOU WILL NEED

1 baked 9-inch square cake,* cooled
2½ cups Butter Cream Frosting
1⅓ cups (about) Baker's Angel Flake Coconut

1 square Baker's Unsweetened Chocolate, melted
White ring-shaped candies
Gumdrops
Paper flag

*For 9-inch square cake, bake *all* of prepared cake mix batter in a greased, floured 9-inch square pan at 325° for 50 to 55 minutes, or until cake tests done.

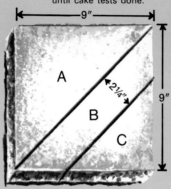

1 Cut cake diagonally in half to make two triangles. From one triangle, cut off a strip 2-1/4 inches wide.

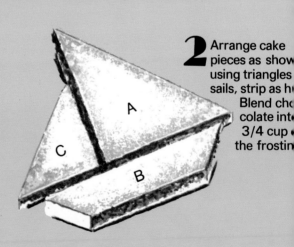

2 Arrange cake pieces as show using triangles sails, strip as h Blend cho colate int 3/4 cup the frostin

3 Spread white frosting on sails; chocolate frosting on hull. Put a line of chocolate frosting between sails as mast. Sprinkle coconut on sails. Arrange candies and flag as shown.

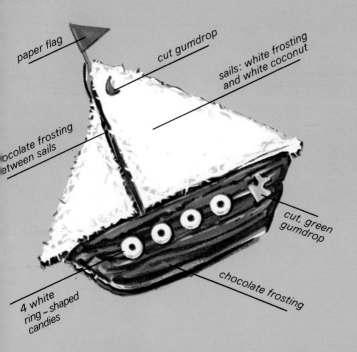

paper flag

cut gumdrop

sails: white frosting and white coconut

chocolate frosting between sails

cut, green gumdrop

chocolate frosting

4 white ring-shaped candies

SANTA

Visions of Toyland take form when Santa
Claus first arrives on the holiday scene.
For a children's holiday party, jolly
Santa Claus Cut-Up Cake is the best
sight of all, and his bagful of goodies
can be enjoyed right away!

Organize a party at a children's orphanage.
Get together with your club group or a number
of friends and arrange to make a pre-Christmas
visit to some youngsters who need cheering.

Check with officials at the selected home to
see what types of items are desired.

Bring materials for making ornaments
including styrofoam shapes, construction
paper, glue sticks, foil, and cotton. Work with
the children making cut-out elves,
angels, reindeer and sleighs.

And don't forget to bring
Santa Cut-Up Cake and some
bright red fruit punch for
refreshment time.

WHAT YOU WILL NEED

1 baked 9-inch square cake layer,* cooled
1 baked 8-inch round cake layer,* cooled
8 cups Seven Minute Frosting
2⅔ cups (about) Baker's Angel Flake Coconut
Red food coloring
Wide black licorice strips
Silver dragées
2 black jelly beans
Black licorice laces
1 red ring-shaped hard candy
1 large red gumdrop

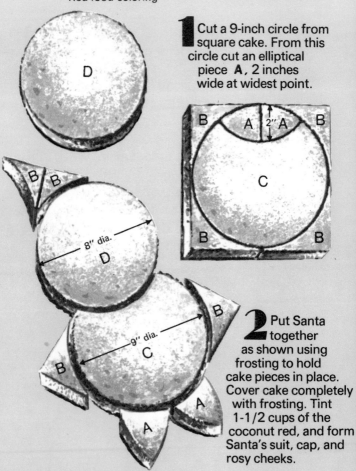

1 Cut a 9-inch circle from square cake. From this circle cut an elliptical piece **A**, 2 inches wide at widest point.

2 Put Santa together as shown using frosting to hold cake pieces in place. Cover cake completely with frosting. Tint 1-1/2 cups of the coconut red, and form Santa's suit, cap, and rosy cheeks.

*Pour 3-1/4 cups prepared cake mix batter into a greased, floured 9-inch square pan and remainder into a greased, floured 8-inch round pan. Bake at 350° for 25 minutes for 8-inch round, 35 minutes for 9-inch square, or until cake tests done.

3 Add untinted coconut trimmings. Decorate with licorice and candy as shown.

cap, suit, beard:
trim with white frosting
white coconut

white frosting

eyes: black jelly beans and black licorice laces

red gumdrop

cut ring-shaped red candy

cap, suit, cheeks: tinted red coconut

belt: wide black licorice strips and silver dragées

boots: black licorice strips

SPACE SHIP

Countdown 5 - 4 - 3 - 2 - 1

Then BLAST OFF for a birthday party that's way ahead of its time. Special for junior astronauts—a make believe trip to the moon. Entry of the Space Ship Cut-Up Cake gets things off to a flying start.

Decorate the party room with cut-out stars and balloons bearing the names of planets.

Clear room space for a moon walk. Place lots of pillows on the floor and then cover them completely with a large sheet. Darken the room and at a given signal, have children remove shoes and walk across the moon-like surface to hunt souvenirs that have been wrapped in foil and sealed with bits of day-glo tape.

After the last crater and valley has been explored, serve refreshments on compartment type foil trays.

WHAT YOU WILL NEED

- 1 baked 13 x 9-inch cake, cooled
- 5⅓ cups Seven Minute Frosting
- 1⅓ cups (about) Baker's Angel Flake Coconut
- 9 small red and white gumdrops

Blue and red sprinkles
Black ribbon licorice
Black licorice laces
Red cinnamon candies
Red stick candy
Small United States flag

1 Cut cake in half lengthwise. Remove 1-inch strip from long side (not used). Finish cutting as shown in diagram.

E E
D
3"
C
3"
C
A
B
center of cake
1"

2 Arrange cake using frosting to hold pieces together. Spread remaining frosting over cake and sprinkle entire cake, except "fins," with coconut.

D
B
A
C E E C

3 Place pieces of ribbon and lace licorice on rocket as shown. Spell out U.S.A. with red cinnamon candies; add "thrust" with red stick candy. Finish decorating with gumdrops dipped in water, and then rolled in red and blue candy sprinkles.

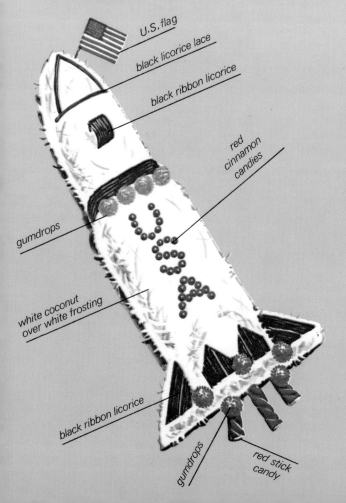

U.S. flag

black licorice lace

black ribbon licorice

red cinnamon candies

gumdrops

white coconut over white frosting

black ribbon licorice

gumdrops

red stick candy

SPORTS

V ✷ I ✷ C ✷ T ✷ O ✷ R ✷ Y !

Cheer for the winners or cheer up the losers. An after-the-game party for those enthusiastic sportsmen is the winning way to good times. Score high with these Sports Page Cut-Ups—show your refreshment strategy.

Instead of the usual tablecloth, prior to party time save the sports pages of your local paper. Tape these together to form correct size. If desired, a quick spray of clear lacquer will add body. Make a list of quiz questions based on the information contained within these pages. Watch the scramble to locate the right answers. Winner could get a pair of tickets to an upcoming local sports event, a game, or an inexpensive T-Shirt which everyone can autograph with a marking pen.

Weather permitting—the best activity of all—go outdoors and play ball!

WHAT YOU WILL NEED

Baked cooled cakes,
  as indicated
Frosting
Baker's Angel Flake
  Coconut

Food coloring
Assorted candies

BASEBALL and MITT

Bake 1-1/2 cups prepared cake mix batter (use 1 package cake mix) in greased, floured 3-cup oven-proof bowl at 325° for 50 minutes. Bake remaining batter in 9-inch round layer pan. Trim layer cake into mitt as diagramed. Using 4-1/2 cups Seven Minute Frosting, first frost mitt; then cover completely with 1-1/3 cups Chocolate-Coated Coconut.

Frost baseball, then cover with 1-1/3 cups coconut. Decorate with red licorice laces, and place on mitt as shown.

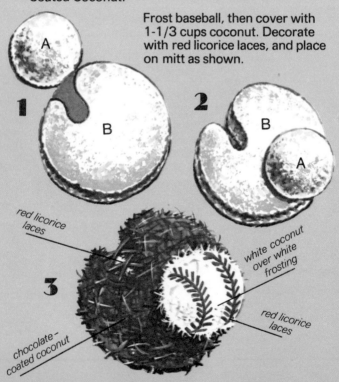

1 A B

2 B A

3
red licorice laces

white coconut over white frosting

red licorice laces

chocolate-coated coconut

FOOTBALL

Bake *all* of prepared cake mix batter (use 1 package cake mix) in a greased, floured 9-inch square pan at 325° for 50 to 55 minutes, or until cake tests done. Cut as diagramed. Frost with 2 cups yellow tinted Four Minute Frosting, mounding up for rounded appearance. Cover generously with 2 cups toasted coconut. Decorate with candy corn, chocolate chips, licorice laces, as shown.

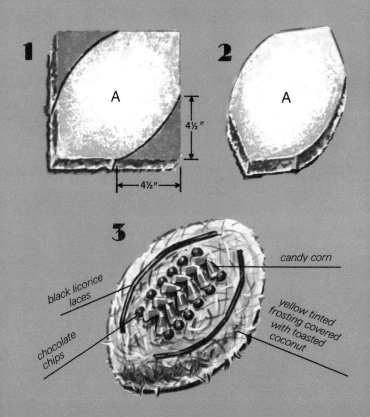

TEDDY BEAR

To a child, happiness is a warm, cuddly Teddy Bear. For one honey of a party that will please tiny tots, reserve a place of honor for Teddy Bear Cut-Up at the Birthday Table.

For decorations, tie a gaily colored personalized balloon to each child's chair and use lots of curly paper streamers on the table.

Plan refreshments that are easy to eat, such as small finger sandwiches cut in different shapes with cookie cutters.

At game time, play Teddy Bear Hunt. Cover little flower pots with foil, plant a sweet treat (a small jar of honey, animal crackers, miniature candy bars, etc.) inside, and hide the gifts about the room. Let the children be guided in their search for these treasures by your hints of "hot" or "cold" or "fuzzy" to keep them on the right trail.

WHAT YOU WILL NEED

- 1 baked 8-inch round cake layer,* cooled
- 1 baked 9-inch square cake,* cooled
- 5⅓ cups Seven Minute Frosting
- 2⅔ cups (about) Baker's Angel Flake Coconut
- 3 squares Baker's Unsweetened Chocolate
- 1 tablespoon butter
- 6 marshmallows
- 3 small round chocolate candies
- 2 large white mints
- 1 large red gumdrop Licorice lace
- 2 chocolate wafers

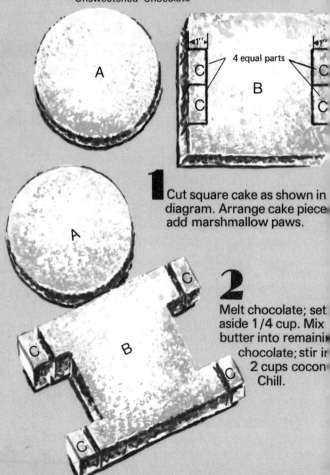

A

B

4 equal parts

C C

C C

1" 1"

1 Cut square cake as shown in diagram. Arrange cake piece add marshmallow paws.

2 Melt chocolate; set aside 1/4 cup. Mix butter into remaini chocolate; stir in 2 cups cocon Chill.

Pour prepared cake batter into pans, filling
each pan to same depth. Bake at 350° for
about 35 minutes, or until cake tests done.

3 Frost face, tummy, and paws with 1-1/3 cups
frosting. Blend reserved chocolate into
remaining frosting; spread over rest of cake.
Sprinkle chocolate coconut on chocolate frosting;
plain coconut on white frosting. Cut chocolate
wafers to fit head as ears, placing marshmallow
under each wafer. Decorate as shown with candy.

ears:
chocolate wafers

chocolate candy
on white candy mint

black gumdrop

black licorice lace

white
frosting
and white
coconut

d
umdrop

chocolate candy

chocolate frosting
and chocolate coconut

hite frosted
arshmallow
with black licorice claws

TIGER

Listen to that Tiger Rrrroar!

Tame teenagers at a Safari Party with a Tiger Cut-Up that purrs. And be ready with a well-fortified refreshment table when this hungry group gets ready to charge.

Set the scene with pith helmets, bongo drums, and if the season is right, an outdoor barbecue. Do a jungle version of Pin the Tail on the Donkey using large pictures or drawings of elephants, lions, or tigers.

Have a marksmanship competition using bow and arrow, darts, or knocking off a set of empty cans using tennis balls.

Play Animal Pantomime. Each person has a chance to imitate the behavior of a particular animal.

Prizes go to the best actor and the fastest guesser.

WHAT YOU WILL NEED

1 baked 9-inch round
    cake layer, cooled
3 baked cupcakes, cooled
2 cups Four Minute
    Frosting, tinted
    orange
1⅓ cups (about) Baker's
    Angel Flake Coconut
½ cup Chocolate-Coated
    Coconut

Red and yellow food
    coloring
2 chocolate wafer
    cookies
1 large marshmallow
1 large black gumdrop
2 large white mints
2 small black candies
1 large red gumdrop
    Black licorice laces

1 Place cake layer on a large tray. Cut cupcakes
in half, vertically; place in pairs, cut side down as
shown to form cheeks and chin.

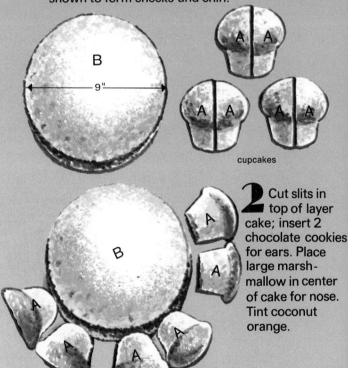

cupcakes

2 Cut slits in
top of layer
cake; insert 2
chocolate cookies
for ears. Place
large marsh-
mallow in center
of cake for nose.
Tint coconut
orange.

3 Frost cake and cupcakes, leaving cookies plain. Build up frosting around marshmallow for 3-dimensional effect. Make stripes with Chocolate-Coated Coconut and orange-tinted coconut. Decorate with candy as shown.

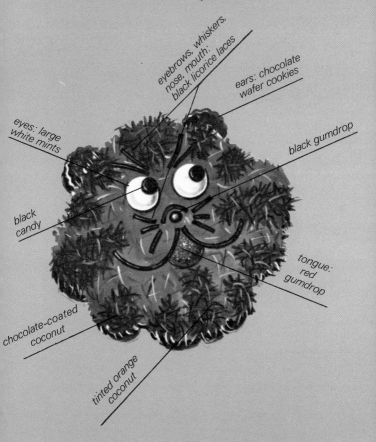

eyebrows, whiskers, nose, mouth: black licorice laces

ears: chocolate wafer cookies

eyes: large white mints

black gumdrop

black candy

tongue: red gumdrop

chocolate-coated coconut

tinted orange coconut

UMBRELLA

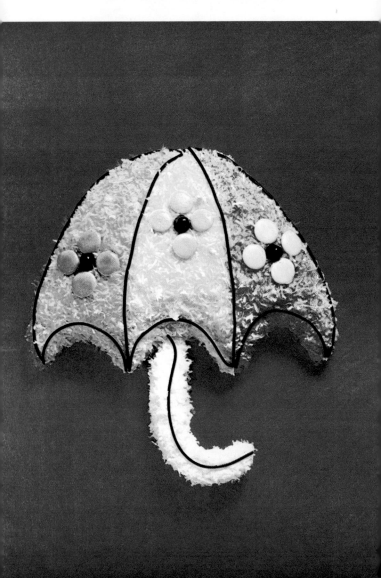

SAY IT WITH A SHOWER!

It's a bridal shower. That special time to fete the bride-to-be. And to set the mood for this outpouring of good wishes and gift giving, what could be nicer than the delicate Umbrella Cut-Up.

Plan a small kitchen-gadget shower and invite guests to come for a pre-shower wrap-hour before the guest of honor arrives. Instead of the usual paper wrappings buy or make a collection of colorful napkins, place-mats, and kitchen towels to hold each gift. Secure with yarn ties.

Melon halves filled with fruit or chicken salad and touched off with a celery stick or pastel-tinted pipe cleaner handle follow the umbrella motif and make a satisfying luncheon or supper menu.

WHAT YOU WILL NEED

1 baked 13 x 9-inch cake, cooled
5⅓ cups Seven Minute Frosting
1⅔ cups Baker's Angel Flake Coconut
Red, green, and yellow food coloring

4 *each* yellow, green, and pink candy mint patties
3 black gumdrops
Black licorice laces

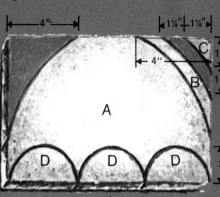

split to make 2 layers

1 Cut cake as diagramed. Split *each* of the three **D**'s through center to form six equal pieces.

2 Arrange pieces **A**, **B**, and **C** on large tray; frost thinly. Position pieces **D** on top of **A** as shown and swirl frosting over entire cake.

3 Tint 1/2 cup coconut pink, 1/2 cup green, and 1/3 cup yellow. Sprinkle on colored coconut as illustrated. Cover the handle with remaining untinted coconut. Decorate with licorice laces and candy as shown.

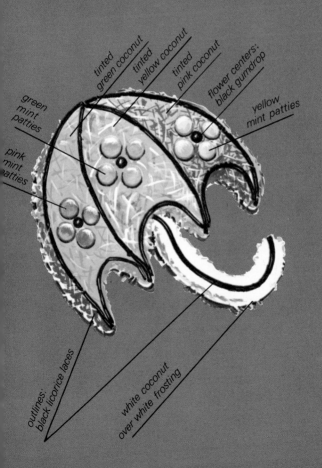

tinted green coconut

tinted yellow coconut

tinted pink coconut

flower centers: black gumdrop

yellow mint patties

green mint patties

pink mint patties

outlines: black licorice laces

white coconut over white frosting

WITCH

Give a hoot and holler then say ALAKAZAM!
It is time for spirits and spells and a little
shim-sham. The Witch Cut-Up minus her
broomstick, but possessing magical charm,
makes the scene on Halloween.

Teens who are beyond the age of trick or
treat will enjoy planning their own
Halloween Party. This is a perfect
time for them to take full responsibility
for shopping, invitations, decorating,
and taking care of clean-up.

If there are any camera buffs in the
crowd, this can be a good opportunity for
some memorable candid shots.

Music, conversation, eating, and drinking
will probably lead the activities. Then there
are some old-fashioned bewitching and
beguiling games that never go out of style —
like bobbing for apples, dancing while
balancing a grapefruit
between foreheads, and
telling ghost stories.

1 baked 9-inch square cake,* cooled

5⅓ cups Seven Minute Frosting, tinted pale yellow

1 cup Baker's Angel Flake Coconut

1 cup Chocolate-Coated Coconut

Yellow and red food coloring

Green gumdrop

Black licorice laces

Black gumdrop

*For 9-inch square cake, bake *all* of prepared cake mix batter in a greased, floured 9-inch square pan at 325° for 50 to 55 minutes, or until cake tests done.

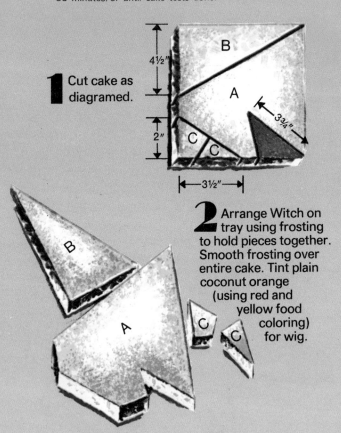

1 Cut cake as diagramed.

2 Arrange Witch on tray using frosting to hold pieces together. Smooth frosting over entire cake. Tint plain coconut orange (using red and yellow food coloring) for wig.

3 Chocolate-Coated Coconut forms peaked hat. Use flattened and cut large green gumdrop for the eye. Decorate with licorice and gumdrop as shown.

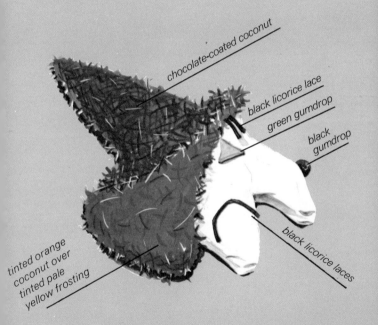

chocolate-coated coconut

black licorice lace

green gumdrop

black gumdrop

black licorice laces

tinted orange coconut over tinted pale yellow frosting

WOOFY DOG

Better than man's best friend is Woofy
Dog Cut-Up, made into the perfect
pet dessert for a children's party.
He'll sit until spoken to, and
won't roll over!

Ask the little guests to bring
their favorite TOY pets along and
have a short animal show. Or, supply simple
drawings of animals and let the children
color and name their works of art.

For a group participation event ask each
child to draw a different part of a dog (legs,
ears, tail, paws) then put them all together.
The breed may not be recognizable, but there
will be lots of giggles over this "created-
to-order" pet.

And what could
be a more welcome
feast than hot dogs?

WHAT YOU WILL NEED

- 1 baked 13 x 9-inch cake, cooled
- 5⅓ cups Seven Minute Frosting
- 1½ cups Baker's Angel Flake Coconut
- ½ cup Chocolate-Coated Coconut
  Red cinnamon candies
- 1 red gumdrop
- 1 black gumdrop
  Black licorice laces

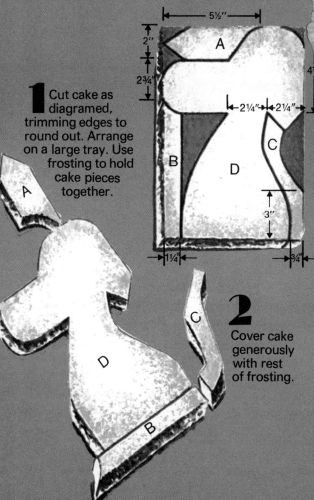

1 Cut cake as diagramed, trimming edges to round out. Arrange on a large tray. Use frosting to hold cake pieces together.

2 Cover cake generously with rest of frosting.

3 Use Chocolate-Coated Coconut to "spot" the dog; then, make him shaggy with 1-1/2 cups coconut. Use flattened red gumdrop for tongue. Add licorice and candies as shown.

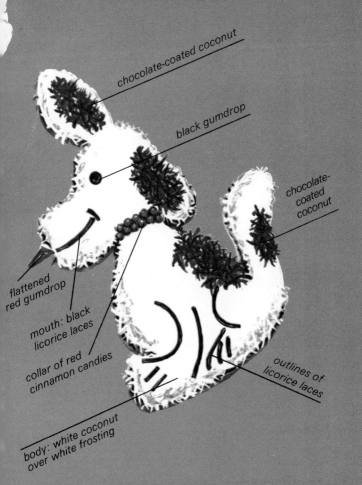

chocolate-coated coconut

black gumdrop

chocolate-coated coconut

flattened red gumdrop

mouth: black licorice laces

collar of red cinnamon candies

outlines of licorice laces

body: white coconut over white frosting